MW01181333

The Gift of Tongues
A doorway to miracles

"...and these signs will accompany
those who believe
...in my name they will speak
in new tongues" (Mk 16:17).

Linda Schubert

Other books by Linda Schubert
Miracle Hour
True Confessions
Miracle Moments
The Healing Power of a Father's Blessing
Precious Power
Miracle Woman Handbook
Miracle Man Handbook
Rich in Mercy

All scripture quotations from the New American Bible

Cover credits
Icon mosaic of Pentecost in the crypt
of the Church of the Dormition,
Mt Zion, Jerusalem, Israel
Used with permission
Cover photo of Theresa Huether and cat Marcy
by Shelly Currin
Computer graphics by Amanda Griffin

Linda Schubert
Miracles of the Heart Ministries
PO Box 4034
Santa Clara CA 95056
Phone (408) 734-8663
Fax (408) 734-8661
www.linda-schubert.com
linda@linda-schubert.com

2nd Printing May 2016
all rights reserved
ISBN 978-1-4507-0575-2

Reader Comments

With simplicity and clarity, Linda Schubert leads us into understanding and treasuring the precious charism of praying in the Holy Spirit. This is a must read for all who desire to pray in tongues and experience the doorway to miracles. Sister Linda Koontz S.N.J.M., Spirit of the Lord International Mission, El Paso TX.

Linda's straightforward explanation of the gift of tongues, accompanied by testimony, will unlock and demystify for its readers this wonderful gift that the Holy Spirit freely gives. Linda is a close friend of the Lamb of God Community and we here in New Zealand know that the fruit of this book will be anointed and without measure. Darren Humphries, Lamb of God Christian Community, New Zealand.

The charism of speaking in tongues is a gift from God that brings our prayer life to a deeper level. Linda makes it seem so inviting; and it is such a needed form of prayer. This book brings the simplicity, the awesomeness, and the wonder of praying in tongues and enables the reader to understand the many facets of this gift. Aggie Neck, Director, Servant House, a Catholic Charismatic House of Prayer, Marksville, LA.

This is an excellent resource to find out all about the gift of tongues— how, where and when to use it. During the last 17 years I have coordinated Life in the Spirit seminars 47 times in the Archdiocese of Vancouver with more than 7,700 participants. At future seminars I will recommend this book to all candidates. Lennie David, Director of Life in the Spirit seminars, Archdiocese of Vancouver, BC Canada.

This book on the gift of praying in tongues is timely and important. Linda Schubert explains the gift of tongues simply, beautifully and profoundly. I am grateful to Linda for her obedience to the Spirit in getting this book into the hands of many. To pray in this language has transformed my life and the lives of my Sisters in our Charismatic Franciscan Religious Congregation. Mother Lucy Lukasiewicz, DLJC, Superior General

Table of Contents

Acknowledgement......................................6

About the cover 7

1. Jesus loves you, this I know 9

2. Listening to love......................................19

3. Tongues then and now.............................27

4. Stories...37

5. Prayer to remove obstacles......................49

6. Prayer to receive tongues 53

7. Tongues in the fabric of your life.............59

8. Closing prayer 69

9. Workshop possibilities 71

10. Resources 75

Acknowledgement

I thought I wouldn't write again. A friend, Nancy, who walked beside me and helped me grow in so many ways, has gone home to the Lord. During our 30 years of friendship we developed a 'project relationship'. I'd get an idea for a little book and she would enthusiastically help bring it to life. So in a special way this is dedicated to Nancy Condon, an encourager par excellence. One of her favorite scriptures was *"...grow in grace and in the knowledge of our Lord and Savior Jesus Christ. To Him be glory now and to the day of eternity. Amen" (2Pt 3:18).*

About the cover

My initial vision for the cover was a doorway in Jerusalem, but when I looked through dozens of photos of doorways, nothing fit. Then I found the icon depicting Pentecost at the Church of the Dormition on Mt. Zion in Jerusalem. This is a *true* doorway into the love and power of the Holy Spirit. Then, I wanted to juxtapose the extraordinary with the ordinary because when we pray in tongues we are not always in holy places, but often walk on ordinary paths filled with the presence and power of God. Wanting to create a sense of connecting heaven and earth, I visualized my friend Theresa holding her kitty, walking around home praying or singing in tongues. And finally, after the cover design took shape, I saw it from one more perspective. I saw Dorothy from *The Wizard of Oz,* trotting down the yellow brick road with little doggie Toto, off to an adventure. This is surely an amazing spiritual adventure.

1

Jesus loves you, this I know

"...hope does not disappoint, because the love of God has been poured out into our hearts through the Holy Spirit that has been given to us" (Ro 5:5).

"Whether these charisms be very remarkable or more simple and widely diffused, they are to be received with thanksgiving and consolation since they are fitting and useful for the needs of the church." (Dogmatic Constitution on the Church #12)

Word List:

Doorway: Opening, gateway, threshold, entrance, means of access.

Miracle: Clearly, without question, only something God can do.

Tongues: Heart to heart, intimate expression with God that goes beyond words, and opens us up to possibilities that are beyond our imagining with known words.

Trust: Assured reliance on the character, ability, strength or truth of someone. One in which confidence is placed.

Charism: A gift given a Christian by the Holy Spirit for the good of the church.

This chapter: The prompting to write about tongues; issues of trust; hearing God's voice; the bridal focus; the Holy Spirit our helper.

People are asking: One day a woman telephoned to order my cassette on tongues from a workshop I conducted in New Zealand years ago. She had participated in a Life in the Spirit seminar, and in an outburst of frustration she exclaimed, "**I don't understand tongues!**" I prayed with her and thought about her concern. Then I received this email from a man: "Can you please elaborate on the origins of the language you speak in your prayer video on YouTube? Is it Latin or Greek? I'm intrigued by it, and would like to know how you have that ability." (I was praying in tongues on a YouTube prayer on my website.)

My response: I want to explore the gift of tongues as a pathway of prayer as I currently understand it. This is a charism that some feel is unnecessary, and they resist it. Many misunderstand its value. Others appreciate the gift and sense it has value, but feel too limited in using it. They want more. Many pray in tongues in limited ways—a few minutes in a prayer meeting, here and there in moments of stress, and then they stop. And then there are the thinkers, the highly intellectual people who analyze it to death. They may even want the gift but they can't get past their heads. Well,

10

from wherever you are, this booklet may help you.

Something to ponder: As I was considering the direction to take, I recalled the scripture about the wedding at Cana (John 2), where Jesus turned the water into wine. He transformed something natural into supernatural. Think about this miracle as you approach tongues. As He turned the water into wine, is He not also taking your natural sounds and bringing them into the supernatural? Water into wine. Something to think about.

My story: I've been praying in tongues since 1977. This gift is a part of the fabric of my life, and a charism I received from the Lord during a tough time in my life following the death of my stepson, Randy. As a Catholic convert I had moved from a position of unformed faith to embracing our beautiful Catholic faith. Then in this time of tragedy I cried out to God for help. Watching a TV program hosted by an evangelist, I made a fresh commitment and asked Jesus to be my Savior and Lord, to baptize me in the Holy Spirit and release in me all the gifts and graces of the Spirit. I asked because I desperately needed my life to work, not because I knew the implications of everything I was asking for. I found myself immersed in the love of God, and crying to Him in a mysterious language. Yet I knew the strange sounds were from my heart to the heart of God. There was such intimacy that I felt like His bride, and He was the bridegroom. And oh, He loved me. The love was so deeply personal, so vibrantly alive, that years of stubborn cynicism melted away. In the weeks and months to come I hungered for scripture, for prayer, for community. Many aspects of my personal life were falling apart, yet something inside felt strong, clean and serene and held very close to the heart of God.

The issue of trust: I realize I'm more able to trust God now. This is important to consider as we approach something unfamiliar, like tongues. Once as I prayed about trust, I heard in my heart: "If you really knew Me you would never fear again. You would always turn to Me. If you would trust Me and entrust to Me all your thoughts, feelings, actions and reactions, I could revitalize your life. I am here to be for you what you need Me to be. I love you so much." Will you talk to God about where you stand on trusting Him? Once I heard the Lord say, "I will take you as far as you want to go. You set the limits." I wondered if I could trust Him enough to remove the limits. Could I? Good question! Can you? *Trust in the Lord with all your heart, on your own intelligence rely not; in all your ways be mindful of him, and he will make straight your paths"* (Prv 3:5-6).

One time in Nigeria: I had just returned to

my local residence in Lagos, following a meeting with 5,000 Nigerians in an open field. Falling to my knees I cried out to God, "The needs are so great, and I am so little." His response melted my heart: "Little in My hands is much." With tears flowing, I responded, "Oh Lord, help me get into Your hands." He seemed to say, "Stay little, surrender into My hands, and watch what I can do." Can we approach the gift of tongues with this same posture of littleness and surrender? *"How numerous have you made, O Lord my God, your wondrous deeds. And in your plans for us there is none to equal you"* (Ps 40:6).

People long to hear God's voice: In the years following my conversion I have written many little Christian books and traveled the world at the invitation of Catholic charismatic groups. Most invitations came as a result of my first prayer booklet, *Miracle Hour,* which has helped countless thousands open to a closer walk with Jesus. People tell me how much they long to hear God speak to them. They deeply desire to trust in His love. The reality of God's love is the deepest truth we can ever know. Opening to and trusting in His love can also help us understand the reason for tongues, because His love is so deep it can take us beyond our normal language, into heavenly realms.

The Lord says, "Let Me hear your voice": I wonder if part of the struggle some people have with tongues is that they are trying to 'make it happen' from the outside, without being up close and open. When I first seriously considered writing about this topic I asked the Lord how to do it. The answer that came was this: "Write it as My bride." (Or spouse.) As He led me to the Song of Songs, I spent time soaking in the intimacy of this portion of scripture. *"...let me hear your voice, for your voice is sweet..."* (Sg 2:14). *"...my friends are listening for your voice, let me hear it"* (Sg 8:13). He wants honest heart-to-heart communication. If we understand this, tongues may open and flow naturally.

What does it mean to be His bride, or spouse? That's something we must each ask Him privately. It may have to do with flowing together, partnership, covenant, trust, and feeling safe and open with Him. There is much more, but He will teach us as we ask. Pray: "Lord, please teach me what it means to be Your spouse." *"...as a bridegroom rejoices in his bride, so shall your God rejoice in you"* (Is 62:5).

Why this kind of help? My first response is that He really loves us. I mean, *really* loves us. Then it hit me: It's all about love. He wants us to reach that level of openness so He can pour

His life through us to help fulfill our destiny. We know from scripture that "*God is love*" (1Jn 4:16) but the impact of this truth doesn't always reach our hearts. Sometimes we receive this only in our heads. When I was released in tongues, and felt God's healing love flowing through the gift, something relaxed deep inside. It was deeply personal and very emotional. I wasn't alone anymore. I was connected. There was a flow of communication that was deep and real. I loved Him and He loved me. And everything looks different through eyes of love.

Why a doorway to miracles? Miracles happen in this relationship as we pray "we" not "me." Jesus and me. Jesus and you. Open your heart to praying as His spouse. (Where are *we* going, Jesus? What are *we* doing here?) Find your own words (in tongues?) and tell Him so. Intimacy with the Lord brings us into the realm of the miraculous. Miracles in the sense that it is clearly, without doubt, only something He could do. *"This is how we know that we remain in him and he in us, that he has given us of His Spirit"* (1Jn 4:13).

The Helper: The Holy Spirit is the Helper, the one who empowers us. God the Father is revealed as the one with overall mastery of everything. Out of His love, everything proceeds. God the Son, Jesus, comes to us as our loving Savior and to reveal and impart the character of God. We invite Him to be Lord of all. The Holy Spirit awakens faith in us. His work is to unite us to Jesus and empower us to live in Him. He guides us through the doorway and helps us get where we need to go. It's time to make friends with Him!

He communes with us (2Cor 13:13).
He comforts us (Jn 14:16).
He intercedes for us (Rom 8:26).
He teaches us (Jn 14:26).
He leads us (Rom 8:14).
He guides us (Jn 16:13).
He empowers our speech (Mk 13:11).
He gives personal sanctification gifts (Is 11:2).
He gives manifestation gifts for service
    (1Cor 12:4-11).
He produces fruit (Gal 5:22-23).

Consider taking different elements of this list and spending time in prayer, communing with Him, reflecting on intercession, gifts, etc. It will help this friendship develop.

Prayer: Thank You, heavenly Father, for loving me, for helping me to pray in a way that fits with my nature. Thank You Jesus for helping me to trust You, to come closer to You, to hear Your voice. Thank You Holy Spirit for being my Helper, my Friend, for opening the door to wonders and miracles. In Jesus' Name I pray. Amen.

It's so timely to see new, fresh material being written about the gifts and charisms of the Holy Spirit. More and more people are hungry for the Lord and are seeking things of the Spirit. The gift of tongues is a charism that people either really want—or really don't want! Once they understand what an awesome and powerful gift it is, they become more open to it. This beautiful little booklet explains the charism of tongues in a way that not only gives understanding, but creates desire. It has given me a new burst of motivation to use my gift of tongues more than I already do! Jolene Carpenter, Catholic Charismatic Renewal Office, Minneapolis, MN

2

Listening to love

"...I will pray with my spirit, but I will also pray with my mind. I will sing praise with the spirit, but I will also sing praise with the mind" (1Cor 14:15).

"My God, if my tongue cannot say in every moment that I love you, I want my heart to repeat it to you as often as I draw breath" (Cure of Ars). (Catechism # 2658)

Word List:

Tongues: Enabled by the Spirit of God, it is an utterance giving audible expression of the spiritual dimension of us to God in prayer so that the believer and/or the community can be edified. (Fr. Peter Sanders)

Baptism in the Holy Spirit: Awakening of unreleased sacraments.

Life in the Spirit seminar: A formation experience; introduction into a life lived in the power and presence of the Holy Spirit.

Charismatic Catholic: A term sometimes used for Catholics who have surrendered to a life changing relationship with Jesus Christ (with or without a Life in the Spirit seminar), and are aware of, and cooperating with, God's desire for an active personal role in every aspect of life. In varying degrees, they are living in the power and presence of the Holy Spirit.

This chapter: Remembering how God has helped us in the past; the movement from formal to personal prayer; charismatic prayer; Life in the Spirit as avenues of renewal; how baptism in the Spirit relates to the sacraments.

Message from Budapest: When I was conducting a healing seminar in Budapest years ago, my translator asked for prayer. He explained, "I want God to wake up my heart!" Do you want that too? The *Catechism of the Catholic Church* says, "Prayer is the life of the new heart. It ought to animate us at every moment." (Catechism #2697) This means prayer encourages us, gives life to us, and gives vigor and zest to us. Let's begin to thank God for the gift and grace of prayer that animates us continually.

Begin by remembering: Consider how the Lord lovingly helped you in the past. I suspect that most of you have experienced the Holy Spirit quietly working in your life more than you realize. You may not have recognized His presence, but nonetheless He has been there for you in countless ways. For example, when you pray heart-to-heart with a friend and you feel a gentle nudge to say something, and then your friend begins to cry. You might feel that moment was guided by the Lord. Well, it probably was. Whispers of possibilities. Thank Him for those precious moments of grace when He was beginning to wake up your heart and take you beyond yourself. Look for ways God is working in you, then take time and acknowledge His presence. "Thank You, Father, thank You Jesus, thank You Holy Spirit, Trinity of Love, for being with me always, in more ways than I have ever appreciated. Help me to recognize Your sweet whispers of possibilities, even in the smallest details of my life."

Whispers of possibilities: I heard about a woman who sat before the Blessed Sacrament in a holy hour, week after week, with her stack of little prayer booklets. One day sitting there, she sighed and put down her books and just started talking to Jesus. "Lord, what do You want me to do?" The thought came quietly into her heart, "Pray for your aunt." And so she did. From there followed a sweet movement from praying other people's prayers, to praying her own prayers. She began to talk to God from her heart, simply and openly. So, from where you are right now, ask Him to release you into prayers from your own heart. *"...where the Spirit of the Lord is, there is freedom"* (2Cor 3:17).

Charismatic prayer: A group of Catholic women invited me to their parish to speak on prayer from the perspective of the Charismatic Renewal. They were unfamiliar with tongues, but interested in learning. I asked both Fr. Bob Faricy and Fr. Peter Sanders to explain charismatic prayer.

From Fr. Bob Faricy, SJ: "I would describe charismatic prayer as prayer directly and clearly inspired by the Spirit, whether in tongues, or inspired prayer out loud, or whatever. It is charismatic prayer when there is little or no doubt that it is directly inspired by the Holy Spirit. Any description or attempt to define charismatic prayer would clearly focus on the Holy Spirit as the initiator and guide."

From Fr. Peter Sanders: "It is prayer that has so many dimensions and types—repentance, thanksgiving, supplication, affirmation, liturgical, intercession, etc. What makes prayer *prayer*, is that it provides a vehicle through which we can enter into relationship with God. Prayer is 'charismatic' when it reaches a dimension of openness to the Spirit of God so as to receive the charisms and/or flow with the Spirit of God in our inner being. Combined with prayer, 'charismatic' would use the gifts of the Spirit in order to define and facilitate the relationship with God."

Story from Philip Middlemiss: When I was fourteen I lived outside of Dunedin, New Zealand, on the Otago Peninsula. There was no public transport to Dunedin so we used bicycles. Much of the trip was off the bike and pushing it over the hills. One day as I came around a corner and opened the Taranaki Gate a new language started. I had no idea what it was, but I knew where it came from. I had read about this in the lives of the saints, as they mentioned their private language with God. Eleven years later I learned the name of this gift when I was baptized in the Holy Spirit.

Something to consider: While Philip and countless others were not 'charismatic' when they were released in tongues, many people are released in tongues through Life in the Spirit seminars (See Chapters 9 and 10), which draw us into the love of God. The more we learn through these seminars, or books that teach this topic, or from people with clear understanding of the process, the more we are able to open our hearts to Jesus. Education can help remove preconceived ideas that have blocked us in the past, and open us to possibilities in the future. Negative or inadequate teaching can block the flow of the Spirit. I attended the seminars after the gift of tongues began to flow, to receive the teaching I desired.

Baptism in the Holy Spirit: Fr. Raniero Cantalamessa, OFM, Cap., preacher to the Holy Father, in his book *Sober Intoxication* (See Chapter 10) helps us understand this concept because people get confused about how baptism in the Holy Spirit relates to sacramental baptism. He speaks of sacramental baptism as unreleased until we say "Yes," because we are baptized as infants without an opportunity to say an adult "Yes." Baptism in the Spirit awakens and releases the Holy Spirit's presence within us through baptism, confirmation and Eucharist. When we say "Yes" something wonderful happens. When we believe, our eyes are opened to see our Lord as living and real and loving us, not simply doctrine or theology.

Fr. Joe's experience: Much of my early formation in charismatic renewal came through Fr. Joe Diebel's teachings and ministry. When I was co-authoring books with Fr. Robert DeGrandis, SSJ many years ago, I interviewed Fr. Joe for a booklet entitled *Coming to Life*. The following interview is recorded in that book: "Fr. Joe, a Jesuit priest/psychologist, was taken to a charismatic prayer meeting. This is a gathering of individuals coming together to praise the Lord, listen to Him and respond with openness. Fr. Joe hid in the back hoping nobody would recognize him. He was negative about the need for baptism in the Holy Spirit. He muttered, 'I'm a priest, I have the Holy Spirit'. Then after observing the people present, he thought, 'These people believe Jesus is right here!' It occurred to him that he had a problem.

Deeply humbled, he whispered, 'Lord I really wish you'd be here when I pray'. As soon as he expressed the desire, He felt God's presence. That changed things for him. Later, in a conversation with his archbishop, Fr. Joe was asked how he was different since being baptized in the Holy Spirit. He replied, 'The difference is that now what I do *works*!'"

Prayer: Thank You heavenly Father, for helping me open to Your love. Thank You for waking up my heart, and reminding me of how you have helped me in the past. Thank You, Jesus, for helping me to move from praying other people's prayers, to praying my own prayers. Thank You Holy Spirit for awakening me to experience more of Your Spirit in my life. In Jesus' Name I pray. Amen.

Linda Schubert leads us in a step-by-step process to help us exercise the gift of tongues in a way that will enrich our spiritual lives. Her quotations from Popes and Church documents give her book a solid footing, and personal testimonies show that this powerful work of the Spirit is of great value for all believers. Kay Murdy, Co-coordinator, Catholic Bible Institute, Los Angeles, CA www.daily-word-of-life.com.

3

Tongues then and now

"When the time for Pentecost was fulfilled, they were all in one place together. And suddenly there came from the sky a noise like a strong driving wind, and it filled the entire house in which they were. Then there appeared to them tongues as of fire, which parted and came to rest on each one of them. And they were all filled with the Holy Spirit and began to speak in different tongues, as the Spirit enabled them to proclaim" (Acts 2:1-4).

"The witnesses who have preceded us into the kingdom, especially those whom the Church recognizes as saints, share in the living tradition of prayer by the example of their lives, the transmission of their writings, and their prayer today..." (Catechism #2683)

Word List:
Pentecost: A Christian feast commemorating the descent of the Holy Spirit on the whole Church.

Prophecy: To speak with divine inspiration.

Application: The use to which something is put.

Tongues: A resource in prayer, taking people beyond the ordinary bounds of speech.

This chapter: The coming of the Holy Spirit at Pentecost; tongues in the early church and tongues now; St. Theresa of Avila and others; varieties of tongues.

Commissioning of the eleven: When He had risen, before the descent of the Holy Spirit at Pentecost, Jesus appeared to the eleven at table, saying to them "... *'Go into the whole world and proclaim the gospel to every creature. Whoever believes and is baptized will be saved...These signs will accompany those who believe: in my name they will drive out demons, they will speak new languages. They will pick up serpents with their hands, and if they drink any deadly thing, it will not harm them. They will lay hands on the sick, and they will recover'"* (Mk 16:15-18).

He promised the power: Jesus promised that when He went home to the Father the Holy Spirit would come. He was releasing the power to go into the whole world. He said in John 14:16, *"I will ask the Father, and he will give you another Advocate to be with you always..."* Then in Acts 1:8, *"...you will receive power when the Holy Spirit comes upon you, and you will be my witnesses...to the ends of the earth."*

The power was released: When the church was born at Pentecost the Apostles and Mary spoke in tongues (Acts 1:13-14), and the power of the Holy Spirit was released in a variety of ways. Miracles and healings abounded; there was power to do amazing things, poured out graces to build the Church. The little gift of tongues seemed to become woven in the fabric of their lives, as the Church spread and grew. Peter and Paul and others led the way.

Peter prayed in the house of Cornelius: When Peter prayed, and the Holy Spirit came upon them, *"...they could hear them speaking strange languages and proclaiming the greatness of God."* And then, *"The circumcised believers who had accompanied Peter were astounded that the gift of the Holy Spirit should have been poured out on the gentiles also, for they could hear them speaking in tongues and glorifying God..."* (Acts 10:45-46).

Paul prayed in Ephesus: *"...when Paul laid hands on them, the Holy Spirit came upon them, and they spoke in tongues and prophesied" (Acts 19:5-6).*

Paul taught the Corinthians and instructed them in right order: *"There are different kinds of spiritual gifts but the same Spirit; there are different forms of service but the same Lord; there are different workings but the same God who produc-*

*es all of them in everyone...to another varieties
of tongues; to another interpretation of tongues"*
(1Cor 12:4-11) and see1Cor 12 to 14.

Varieties of tongues

*"...they were all filled with the Holy Spirit and
began to speak in different tongues, as the Spirit
enabled them to proclaim"* (Acts 2:4).

Different tongues: Each person had a unique
language of tongues, with a variety of different
applications.

Anointing on the ears of the hearer: Individuals spoke in tongues (in their own language
of the Spirit) and the listeners were foreigners of
many lands. Each heard the message in his own
language. *"Now there were devout Jews from every nation under heaven staying in Jerusalem.
At this sound (tongues) they gathered in a large
crowd, but they were confused because each one
heard them speaking in his own language ..."*
(Acts 2:5-7).

As an interesting aside, Carol, a Catholic
friend, told me of a time when she was speaking
to a Spanish group in the Caribbean. She asked
for an interpreter and they said it was not neces-
sary, because she was speaking the local Spanish
dialect perfectly. She didn't know Spanish. In this
case she was speaking in English, not tongues,

but they heard it in Spanish. This seemed to be an experience of anointing on the ears of the hearer. Nobody could explain it. Also, David Mangan has had experiences with tongues similar to those in the early church, which you will find in his interesting book referenced in Chapter 10.

Speaking in tongues with interpretation: There is the phenomenon of speaking publicly in tongues and having someone else understand and express the meaning of the tongues. This includes the charism of interpretation, and seems to mirror the gift of prophecy, according to Fr. Peter Sanders. *"...one who speaks in a tongue should pray to be able to interpret"* (1Cor 14:13).

Praying in tongues for personal edification: *"Whoever speaks in a tongue builds himself up..."* (1Cor 14:4). Tongues, individually or in a group, as a personal prayer resource without needing interpretation, seems to be a part of the Church, then and now. (See also Ro 8:26-27 and Jude 20.)

Singing in the Spirit: This is praying in tongues in song. *"Let the word of God dwell in you richly, as in all wisdom you teach and admonish one another, singing psalms, hymns, and spiritual songs with gratitude in your hearts to God"* (Col 3:16).

Other names for tongues: In the formative years of the church there have been many references to *spontaneous prayer without words*, closely resembling tongues. Sometimes it was called *jubilation*, or *ecstatic utterances*, and it was taking people beyond the ordinary bounds of speech into the realm of the Spirit. Today, people sometimes call it *praying in tongues, praying in the Spirit*, or *praying in their heavenly language*, or simply their *private language with God*.

**

Saints through the ages: There are stories told of St. Ignatius weeping in mass and he started to say something and it made no sense. Tears came and he called it tongues. Stories are told about St. John Vianney praying in tongues when hearing confessions. It is said that he then knew the hearts of the penitents. And there are references here and there of many saints, including St. Anthony of Padua and St. Paul of the Cross, St. Dominic and others and more recently Padre Pio, speaking in various tongues, speaking in foreign languages without having been learned, or ecstatic utterances. The following is the only specific documentation I have.

St. Theresa of Avila: This Doctor of the Church, a 16th Century nun, a close friend of St.

John of the Cross, has this to say in her classic *The Interior Castle* (in the 6th mansion, chapter 6, paragraphs 11 and 15): "Our Lord sometimes causes in the soul a certain jubilation and a strange and mysterious kind of prayer. If He bestows this grace on you, praise Him fervently for it; I describe it so that you may know that it is something real. I believe that the faculties of the soul are closely united to God but that He leaves them at liberty to rejoice in their happiness together with the senses, although they do not know what they are enjoying nor how they do so. This may sound nonsense but it really happens."

Then paragraph 15: "May His Majesty often grant us this kind of prayer which is most safe and beneficial; we cannot acquire it for ourselves as it is quite supernatural…"

Through the ages: Tongues as a powerful resource in prayer may have been present in various applications and degrees throughout church history with many of the known saints and hidden faithful. Many leaders believe the charisms of the Holy Spirit are one of the ways the Lord has continually provided to help build the Church. And the little gift of tongues seems to be a part of the fabric of that growth. *"Pursue love, but strive eagerly for the spiritual gifts, above all that you may prophesy. For one who speaks in a tongue* *does not speak to human beings but to God, for no one listens; he utters mysteries in spirit. ..Whoever speaks in a tongue builds himself up…Now I should like all of you to speak in tongues, but even more to prophesy. One who prophesies is greater than one who speaks in tongues, unless he interprets, so that the church may be built up"* (1Cor 14:1-5).

A reality ever alive

"The Spirit dwells in the Church and in the hearts of the faithful, as in a temple… and unifying her in communion and in the works of ministry, he bestows upon her varied hierarchic and charismatic gifts, and in this way directs her; and he adorns her with his fruits (cf. Eph. 4:11-12; 1 Cor. 12:4; Gal. 5:22). (Lumen Gentium #4)

Pope John Paul II: "The emergence of the Renewal following the Second Vatican Council was a particular gift of the Holy Spirit to the Church." (Address to the ICCRO Council March 14, 1992)

His Holiness Benedict XVI: In an address to the participants at the meeting of Catholic Fraternity of Charismatic Covenant Communities and Fellowships October 31, 2008: "What we learn in the New Testament on charisms, which appeared as visible signs of the coming of the Holy Spirit, is not a historical event of the past, but a reality ever alive. It is the same divine Spirit, soul of the Church, that acts in every age and those mysterious and effective interventions of the Spirit are manifest in our time in a providential way."

Patti Mansfield: In her book, *As By A New Pentecost* (See Chapter 10), Patti Gallagher Mansfield recounts how a group of students from Duquesne University in Pittsburgh were baptized in the Spirit on a retreat weekend in 1967. This retreat, known as the Duquesne Weekend, marked the beginning of the Charismatic Renewal in the Catholic Church. She says, "I am not a foundress, but a witness to the great grace of being baptized in the Holy Spirit." During that weekend many of the retreatants were baptized in the Holy Spirit and experienced gifts of the Spirit. She continued, "I know that if an ordinary person like me could experience the love of God in this way, anyone could come to know His love."

Quoting Patti in Dave Mangan's book (see Chapter 10), "From the first Pentecost on, the Holy Spirit has always come in response to fervent prayer…Pope Leo XIII was urged to call the entire Church to pray more fervently to the Holy Spirit…and at Duquesne they asked with the same fervor, 'Divine Spirit, renew your wonders in this our day as by a new Pentecost'."

Dave Mangan: In his book, *God loves you and there is nothing you can do about it*, he comments on his experience on the Duquesne weekend: "By education and career I am a mathematician and I tend to begin my approach to any issue with reasoned logic." He reflected on his sacraments of baptism and confirmation; he listened to the talks; and thought about how he could respond to God's initiative. It occurred to him to pray for a renewal of his confirmation. You may want to read his book for details on what happened next! (See Chapter 10.)

Prayer: Thank You heavenly Father, for Your love poured out, then and now. Thank You for the mighty work of Pentecost, and the gift of tongues in the early Church. Thank You for allowing us to know about St. Theresa of Avila's experience with tongues. Thank You, Jesus, for allowing us to participate today in the gifts of Pentecost. Thank You Holy Spirit, for the amazing experiences at Duquesne University, and the renewal poured out from that time. In Jesus' Name I pray. Amen.

4

Stories

"Hear now, all you who fear God, while I declare what He has done for me" (Ps 66:16).

"Even before activity, mission means witness and a way of life that shines out to others." (Redemptoris Missio #26 John Paul II)

Word List:
Tongues: A gift of prayer given by the Holy Spirit; an intimate connection where we collaborate with the Holy Spirit, in unison with Him to bring forth God's purpose. (Fr. Peter Sanders)
Purpose: Objective, expected outcome, intended result.
Testimony: First hand authentication of a fact; evidence; witness.

This chapter: Stories to help us understand more about the gift of tongues.

A man who argued with God about tongues: A man named Bob was given a testimony booklet I wrote many years ago in which I mentioned praying in tongues. He was resisting the concept of tongues as he was getting ready to go to work one morning. Standing in the bathroom, he muttered, "Lord, anything but tongues!!" Then as he was brushing his teeth the Lord spoke to him: "Bob, I have talked to you all these years in *your* language. Won't you talk to Me now in *mine*?" Bob laughed and cried and surrendered. He was released in tongues as toothpaste ran down his cheek.

My experience in India: In Kerala, South India, I was asked at the last minute before leaving a series of meetings, to speak with a group of several thousand people, with an interpreter, at 7:00 a.m., for an hour, with no advance preparation. I prayed earnestly in tongues for guidance. The moment I stepped to the microphone, I heard the Lord saying in my heart, "Now do this next…do this next…do this next." He carried me through the hour. So much love! *"Whoever speaks in a tongue builds himself up…"* (1Cor 14:4). As I prayed in tongues the Holy Spirit showed me what to do in a challenging situation. I grew in trust.

A teachable moment in Malta: Another time when I was conducting a charismatic women's retreat on the Island of Malta, I stopped what I was saying, faltered, and began to pray in tongues. A woman in the front row called out, "I know why you are doing that." When I questioned her she responded, "Because you don't know what to do next!" We all had a good laugh. It was a teachable moment for those women interested in understanding the purpose of tongues. And in fact as I prayed the Lord showed me exactly what to do next!

She listened and knew how to pray: I visited a friend in a Carmelite monastery one time. She was well versed in the ministry and work of the Holy Spirit, and asked me to talk to the Lord about my future in tongues, and 'she would listen'. What a novel idea, I thought. Then as I began to pray in tongues, with a specific focus on my unknown future, the Lord showed her exactly how to pray for me. There was such clarity and power in sister's prayer. The process gave me increased understanding of the rich scope of this form of prayer.

My mother's experience: When my dad was very ill, mom prayed, "Lord, show me how to pray if I see Charlie dying." And when he went into crisis she said, "I immediately prayed softly in my heavenly language and he was restored to normal."

When dad was dying: He was in a coma, and was dying. I sat at his bedside and prayed in the

Spirit for an hour. Because our relationship had unresolved issues, I was especially praying for completion of unfinished business between us. As I prayed, a holy presence came into the room, and my father spoke from his spirit to my spirit. A person in the room would not have heard a whisper. He said, "I'm sorrrrrrryyyyyyyy!" Those words traveled some 40 years back to a hurting little girl. I said to his silent form, "I forgive you, daddy." The next day Jesus took my dad home. As I prayed in tongues my father, although in a coma, heard something that touched him deeply. What was going on in my spirit through the Holy Spirit, connected with his spirit, causing him ask forgiveness.

Shelly Currin's story: With Linda's mentoring, I had been working on developing more discipline with praying in tongues. This included praying for longer periods of time and trying new things like singing more freely and allowing different 'vocabularies' to come forth as I expressed different emotions in my prayer language. On the long drive home from dropping my son off at Boy Scout camp, I decided to practice these new things by praying in tongues. Nobody would hear me. I sang in tongues to instrumental music. The prayer changed focus a few times, including worship, spiritual warfare, and intercession. Sometimes pure joy filled my heart and sometimes deep pain with tears. A few times I could hear Linda's voice in my mind saying, "Press on, keep going," and that would give me fresh energy.

There was breakthrough in many areas, new freedom in my prayer language and, I'm sure, work done in heaven from the intercession. After about two hours a significant breakthrough came. For years I wanted to write my testimony of God's healing. Suddenly, as I drove along the freeway, the words for the beginning of that testimony came clearly into my mind. I pulled off the road and wrote it down. Those two hours of praying in tongues were a milestone in my spiritual life. It takes discipline to pray for long periods. Like running a marathon, you don't run 26 miles without training. The same is true of praying in tongues for extended times. With the help of the Holy Spirit, we have to build up the "prayer muscles" and train for endurance. When we do, the Holy Spirit will do amazing things. (Shelly's testimony booklet was birthed in tongues, and is referenced in Chapter 10.)

Theresa Huether's story: One Friday afternoon I was crossing a bridge over the creek that runs through the high school campus where I work. I was looking down on the water when scores of teenagers came streaming past me on their way home. Seeing each face my heart began to stir with a profound gratitude for them. The feelings turned into compassion and awareness of their vulnerability, fear, and pain. I wanted to cry out to God to help them be happy and free. Mere English words couldn't express what my heart was crying for. Using tongues allowed me to let the Spirit of God pray through me, praying for them.

If I had been limited to my own English language I couldn't say all I needed to say. Praying in tongues took all that was in my heart and placed it in God's heart. I didn't know what each young person needed. Using my prayer language, I let the Holy Spirit pray it for me— absolutely perfectly. I could look each one in the face while praying under my breath, knowing God would hear from my heart the precise petition needed for each. Then I left them in His hands, and continued on my way in peace. (Theresa is the woman on the book cover, and also has a testimony booklet referenced in Chapter 10.)

From Carolyn Suty: The story I have is about receiving one word of my prayer language when I was baptized in the Holy Spirit. I used this one word in prayer for several months and then a lady prayed for me and I received a full flow. I asked God for years why I only received one word and what I felt in my spirit was that He was healing something very deep within me that I wasn't even aware of. Praying in tongues edifies us according to the word. He knew just what I needed. The second reason was to settle in my heart that God does not operate on formulas. I often pray for people to receive their prayer language and am comfortable if they receive one word, two words or sing their prayer language. He is a powerful God who gives gifts the way He knows is best.

From Lennie David: I met Betty 20 years ago in my parish, Immaculate Conception, Delta, BC. In a clear voice the Lord asked me to lay hands on her. I was hesitant because she was a stranger, but as I believed that obedience is better than sacrifice, I asked this lady if I could pray for her. She enthusiastically said 'yes'. I started using my heavenly language not knowing the kind of prayers that were needed. She started crying and told me it was her birthday and that she had prayed she would meet someone who knew, loved, and served the Lord. At this point I lit a candle for her intentions, all the while praying in tongues.

Becoming good friends, I invited her to attend our annual retreat. She gladly accepted. Within nine months, she told me she was being called by the Lord to join a convent. After entering a contemplative Benedictine order, Pope

John Paul II invited these nuns to be his intercessors at Monastero Mater Ecclesace in the Vatican. Sister Maria Gabriel (her new name) was one of eight chosen from around the world for this special assignment. She served both Pope John Paul and Pope Benedict, and has just finished a five year term.

Without using the gift of tongues, I would not have known exactly what it was that I had to pray for Sister Maria Gabriel. These days I use it as a powerful means of intercession.

Darren Humphries in New Zealand: My son Elijah died several years ago from seizures related to a genetic condition. He sustained major brain damage and organ failure. In his last thirty minutes of life with him in my arms and surrounded by family and close friends, we prayed out our hearts together in tongues. The peaceful presence of the Lord filled the room. Elijah walked with his Lord into his inheritance. At a time when there were no natural words, our lips were filled with tongues, of praise to God, of the deepest groaning of our hearts, returning to the Lord the life of our son and brother. The parish priest, observing this, was amazed at our ability to pray in this way.

From Sr. Linda Koontz: One day I felt an urgency to pray for my father. Although I didn't know what it was about, I immediately stopped what I was doing and prayed for 45 minutes in tongues. I learned later that he was in a terrible accident on a rural country road at that exact time, and sustained serious injuries. A young man found him there and took care of him so that he didn't go into shock and die.

Let the little children come: Dave Mangan developed Life in the Spirit programs for youth. When his fourth child, David, age five, attended a session, he too received the gift of tongues. Dave did not include two year old Ann in the program, feeling that she was too young. What happened the next day, however, changed his mind. After his morning kindergarten session, young David was playing with Ann in the basement. His father overheard David telling Ann about the love of Jesus and asked her if she wanted more of Jesus in her life. When she said yes, he led her in a simple prayer asking for the Holy Spirit. Then he said, "Talk like this," and he began to pray in tongues. So did Ann. That was more than twenty years ago and has clearly born much fruit. In his book (see Chapter 10) Dave says: "If a five year old can pray for a two year old and bear fruit, I think it's safe to say that this is not rocket science. All we need is simple faith."

From Arlene Apone in Detroit: One afternoon while shopping at Lowe's I heard a horrible scream and then a woman's wailing. Walking toward the sounds, I saw a man laying on the floor and a woman being restrained by another woman. Several employees gathered around the scene and a nurse knelt down by the man's side and tried to get a pulse. There apparently was none. It looked as if the man had a heart attack and expired. The emergency team was called and crowds gathered. The wife continued to scream and wail.

Instinctively I went down on my knees about 20 feet away from the man on the floor and began to pray in the Spirit. I knew I was interceding but had no knowledge of pleading for this man's life. I simply and quietly prayed in the Spirit. After about ten minutes the man's knee rose up and color came back into his chalky white face and hands. The shocked nurse got a pulse and the man's wife fell to her knees beside her husband. The emergency team arrived. I got up and went on my way thanking God who chose to bring life back to this man. No one realized I was praying, but I believe God used me in a strange situation and brought this man back to life. Through this unique experience, I can relate to those who have seen the dead raised to life. God's power continues to flourish through His charisms. Let us never doubt or fail to use them in all the situations of life. Glory to God!

Gabriele Sedda, London: "When I was baptized in the Holy Spirit I wanted to receive the gift of tongues, so I bought the book *Praying in Tongues* by Fr. Bob DeGrandis. I started praying every day for the gift. Nothing happened for a few months, and I was getting cross with God about it. Then one evening as I was home praising God and ironing, I realized I was actually praying in tongues. Since then I have never looked back. I also realize I have a different tongue if I am praising, interceding, etc. One time I was at the Westminster Prayer Group in London, praying for healing in tongues for a young woman from Jordan. She heard me speaking her language, and as a result she was healed. When she asked me to repeat it, I replied I did not know what I said."

Prayer: Thank You heavenly Father, for helping me to know that tongues is Your language. Thank You, Father, for all the stories of Your people opening to Your gifts and walking on grace filled paths. Thank You, Jesus, for showing me that the gifts are not formulas, but flow out of relationship with You. Thank You, Jesus, for the amazing things that can come out of the mouths of little children. Thank You, Jesus, for showing me that I can be a link in the chain of prayer to accomplish Your will—whether it is for fathers in accidents on lonely roads, dying fathers, and dying sons, high school children, strangers on the floor in a home improvement store, or breakthrough to become writers. Thank You, Holy Spirit, for continuing to pour out Your Spirit on me now as I seek a closer walk with You. In Jesus' Name I pray. Amen.

This little book carries a wonderful invitation to receive your prayer language. Linda's warm comments invite you to share in the gift that strengthens the believer, opens the door to the supernatural and communicates directly to the Holy Spirit. I believe it will be a valuable tool for the body of Christ. Carolyn Suty is a speaker and retreat leader for Catholic and ecumenical groups and works with Aglow International.

5

Prayer to remove obstacles

"Follow the way of love and eagerly desire spiritual gifts…" (1Co 14:1).

"…when we pray, do we speak from the height of our pride and will, or 'out of the depths' of a humble and contrite heart? (Ps 30:1). …humility is the foundation of prayer. Only when we humbly acknowledge that 'we do not know how to pray as we ought' (Rom 8:26) are we ready to receive freely the gift of prayer…" (Catechism #2559)

Word List:
   Tongues: A private language with God.
   Repentance: To turn from sin and dedicate oneself to the amendment of life; to change one's mind.
   Obstacle: Something that impedes progress or achievement.
   Cleanse: To rid of impurities.
   Forgiveness: To give up resentment or claim to requital for; to cancel a debt.

This chapter: Prayer of repentance, healing and surrender and release of the Holy Spirit.

Receive the Gift: At Pentecost, Peter made an eloquent speech about the crucified Lord who died for their sins, which cut the listeners to the heart, and they asked what they should do. Peter responded, *"...Repent and be baptized, every one of you, in the name of Jesus Christ for the forgiveness of your sins; and you will receive the gift of the Holy Spirit"* (Acts 2:37-38). Turning from sin and changing one's life is an issue of the heart. Repentance and baptism are graces for the humble, as we become little and draw near. Our Lord wants an intimate heart relationship with us, no walls. We hide when we feel guilty. *"But when the kindness and generous love of God our savior appeared, not because of any righteous deeds we had done but because of his mercy, he saved us through the bath of rebirth and renewal by the Holy Spirit, whom he richly poured out on us through Jesus Christ our savior…"* (Ti 3:4-6). So much love! *"All bitterness, fury, anger, shouting and reviling must be removed from you, along with all malice. Be kind to one another, compassionate, forgiving one another as God has forgiven you in Christ"* (Eph 4:31-32).

Prayer of repentance and healing

Lord, I know that repentance is an act of love. Show me how to prepare for more of You. I am deeply sorry for the times I have been unfaithful to You. I repent of lack of trust. For the times You have invited me to draw me near and I resisted, I am truly sorry. For the times You have asked me to do something and I didn't do it, please forgive me. I am sorry for neglecting prayer, for going my own way, and for all disobedience. I am sorry for the times I've used my tongue to harm and not to heal. I am sorry for my independence, my pride, my selfishness. I am sorry for judging other people, and especially for judging the spirituality of others. I repent of cynical thoughts about praying in tongues.

Lord I bring You all my negative feelings and memories that block the flow of Your love. Help me to release to You the hurts I am carrying from other people that restrict my freedom today. Help me repent of the ways I have blocked my own freedom because of sin. I choose to forgive all who have hurt me. As a person becoming healed I will keep my heart soft and open with self forgiveness and forgiving others. I take the responsibility for my life and recognize that when You ask me to do something You give me the grace to do it. Thank You Lord. Amen.

Prayer of surrender and release of the Holy Spirit

Lord Jesus I surrender to You today with all my heart and soul. Please come into my heart in a deeper way. I say 'Yes' to You today. I open all the secret places in my heart to You and say 'Come on in'. Jesus You are Lord of my whole life. I believe in You and receive You as my Lord and Savior. I hold nothing back. Thank You for the Holy Spirit. Stir up Your Spirit in me. Baptize me with Your Holy Spirit. I want to discover and use Your gifts; I want to receive all You desire to give me. (Continue in your own words.) Thank You Lord. In Jesus' Name. Amen.

Repent, forgive, and watch His Spirit move!

6

Prayer to receive tongues

"If you then…know how to give good gifts to your children, how much more will the Father in heaven give the Holy Spirit to those who ask him?" (Lk 11:13).

"The Holy Spirit who teaches the Church and recalls to her all that Jesus said also instructs her in the life of prayer, inspiring new expressions of the same basic forms of prayer: blessing, petition, intercession, thanksgiving, and praise." (Catechism #2644)

Word List:

Tongues: Praying beyond words in the language of the Spirit.

Desire: Have a longing for; strong intention or aim; conscious impulse toward something that promises satisfaction in its attainment.

Ask: To make a request of; to seek to obtain by making your wants known.

Expect: Anticipate or look forward to the coming of; preparing for; assurance that what you are looking for will be fulfilled.

Receive: To come into possession of; admit; welcome; greet.

This chapter: Preparing to receive, how to receive, receiving (or releasing) the gift of tongues.

A nun in Canada: When I was conducting a day of renewal in Toronto with about 300 people, at one point we all began to sing in tongues. It flowed like a symphony for an extended time. During the break a nun came up to me and said, "I was standing in the back when the group was singing in tongues. It was so beautiful, that I just joined in." The Lord released her in tongues as the group sang in the Spirit in free harmony. Maybe you have been 'standing in the back'. Is it time to join in?

Free will: God's love always gives us free will. We start and stop at our own volition; it is voluntary participation. That said, it is beautifully interactive with the Holy Spirit so 'think we'.

What does tongues sound like? We make sounds that come from an inner place, sounds that are not a learned language, with each unique to the individual. It is something deep in the soul reaching to the heart of God, sometimes sounding like groaning. Paul writes, *"...the Spirit too comes to the aid of our weakness; for we do not know how to pray as we ought, but the Spirit itself intercedes with inexpressible groanings"* (Rom 8:26). In the beginning it could even sound like baby talk or babble, or nonsense. But it is not nonsense. It is our own love language. Someone sent me a humorous quotation: "Be yourself. Everyone else is already taken." My prayer language is not the same as yours, and yours is not mine. We don't copy others, although in a workshop we might imitate a leader for a moment or two to get moving. (Like the five year old telling the two year old, 'talk like this'.)

Get ready: The natural precedes the spiritual. In scripture miracles were preceded by human acts. Moses threw down his rod before it turned into a snake. Joshua marched around Jericho seven times before the walls came down. Peter stepped out of the boat before he walked on water. The same principle applies in receiving tongues. Start speaking and God's Spirit comes. It won't happen with your mouth closed. (It's hard to steer a parked car.) Some wait with their mouth open waiting for God to move it. Others hold their mouth closed expecting the Lord to open it. He waits for you to make a move.

Get set: God is generous with His gifts. To receive, you welcome it humbly with a conscious exercise of faith. Ask God for the gift, open your mouth expectantly and speak in faith what God has placed there. You remain in control; speak when you want to speak and stop when you want to stop. Because it is unlike any other experience you don't know what it means to do it; you don't know how to begin. So, take a moment and practice making starter sounds, to loosen your tongue.

Go! Open your mouth and begin to speak. Jesus turned the water into wine at Cana. He will turn your natural sounds into a heavenly language as you begin. Open your mouth and just do it. Don't analyze the sounds as they come, just let them flow. Relax, and enjoy the spiritual adventure. Use the following prayer as a starter, but then move into tongues.

"Holy Spirit, come. Please guide my prayer. As I open my mouth and begin to speak, let Your Spirit form the meaning. I come to You in humble trust and ask You to release in me the gift of praying in tongues. I need a private language with You. You in me and I in You. I need words to praise You, to thank You for who You are and what You do for me. I need... (add your own words). Come Holy Spirit and help me express in tongues the things You want to express. Bring forth the response You want. Thank You for awakening this charism in me and helping me take it where You want it to go." (Begin to express things to Him in tongues. As you move your mouth and make starter sounds, His Spirit will get involved and draw you forward into a language of the Spirit. Keep going. Louder. Don't whisper. Turn your heart to Him and continue to pray, but not in your known language.)

Or sing: Sing in tongues to a known melody first. Or, if you don't know Spanish, or Chinese, etc., turn on a foreign language station and sing in tongues as they sing in their language.

Gratitude: Take some time and thank the Lord for this new way of praying. Even if you have only received a couple of syllables, return it to Him with gratitude, which releases faith and will help increase the gift in greater power. *"Thanks be to God for his indescribable gift"* (2Cor 9:15).

Praying in tongues is like breathing to me. It gives me the grace to go through every moment of my life. I can testify that all that is shakable has been shaken in my life. The strength, peace and revelation that God breathes into me as I pray in tongues sustains me. Linda's book is a timely prompting from heaven to awaken us to the power of tongues so that we can be victorious in every situation. Barbara Anne Moore, Speaker and Advisor for Magnificat International Ministry to Women.

7

Tongues in the fabric of your life

"But you, beloved, build yourselves up in your most holy faith; pray in the Holy Spirit" (Jude 20).

"The Holy Spirit, whose anointing permeates our whole being, is the interior Master of Christian prayer. He is the artisan of the living tradition of prayer. To be sure, there are as many paths of prayer as there are persons who pray, but it is the same Spirit acting in all and with all. It is in the communion of the Holy Spirit that Christian prayer is prayer in the Church." (Catechism #2672)

Word List:
   Tongues: A devotional resource.
   Amazing: Filled with wonder.
   Potential: Filled with latent possibilities.
   Edify: To instruct or improve spiritually. To build, establish, instruct, enlighten, to give spiritual insight, gain comprehension of a problem, to cause to grow.
   To heal: To reconcile, to make straight, to mend, cleanse, rehabilitate, improve.

This chapter: Tongues as a devotional resource to help in daily life

More thoughts from Fr. Peter: He reminds us that "Tongues released and matured can be used in a variety of contexts." And, "Using—and using maturely—the gift of tongues will enable you to cross over the threshold into the house of spiritual gifts so you can have much freer access to that which is in the house."

Many spiritual gifts: There are the most commonly known sanctification gifts of Isaiah 11:2, the charismatic gifts of 1Corinthians 12, and a study of the New Testament will reveal many other gifts of ministry and service. Mature use of tongues can help us enter into the rich variety of gifts the Lord has available for His people. Tongues as a way to begin and receive other charisms, can be interwoven in the fabric of your life.

Some forms of tongues:

Easy tongues: Chatting with God about everyday life.

Battle tongues: A strong tongues where you have a sense of battling for something.

Intercessory tongues: Also can be a sense of battle, fighting for God's kingdom to come and reign over a situation.

Praise tongues: A different sound will come

as you lift your voice to heaven in praise of our mighty God.

New tongues: Depending on the focus, your tongues can vary considerably.

Various thoughts

ABC: Always be careful. Always invite the Holy Spirit to guide your tongues, and then give it to Him at the close of the session. Always place the gift under His protective care.

Listen: When you pray in tongues, listen. Things will come to mind that you need to know. Be attentive to your thoughts and feelings as you pray. Ask for insight on various issues, and then listen for the answer. You will be amazed at the help He is ready to give you.

Arlene on listening: I've often reflected on this gift of tongues as the language of the Kingdom of God. As an empowered and holy communication, we can do more than speak in tongues. We can, I believe, listen in tongues. When listening, if I pray quietly and inwardly in tongues I seem to hear the Other better. I believe the Holy Spirit within gives this blessing. *"For 'who has known the mind of the Lord, so as to counsel him?' But we have the mind of Christ"* (1Co 2:16). Arlene Apone, Catholic Charismatic Renewal Center, Detroit.

Ask: Lord, why am I feeling this way? How should I respond to this situation? Then pray in tongues and listen. Ask for discernment. When we ask, we make room for an answer. Simple, but profound.

Distractions: Don't worry. When they come, mentally hand them to the Lord and keep going. Or, ask Him if it is something He is bringing to mind, not a real distraction. Be attentive.

In and out naturally: Pray with the Spirit and with understanding. Pray in and out of tongues and mental prayer. Bring scripture into your prayer. Dig deeper. *"...I will pray with my spirit, but I will also pray with the mind; I will sing with the spirit, but I will also sing with the mind"* (1Cor 14:15).

Not mindless chatter: Tongues is not mindless rambling. It might be focused on praising God, intercession, coming against negative forces, facing battles, what to do about your future, or a variety of personal issues. Being present to the Lord as you pray is important. "...it is most important that the heart should be present to him to whom we are speaking in prayer..." (Catechism #2700)

Focus: Bring important issues to the Lord in tongues. Combine it with scripture. How to do that? Focus. You will understand, when the gift is released and beginning to flow in you. It's amazing the depth of inner healing that will come as you target specific areas in tongues. It goes to the very root of the problem, which Jesus knows even if you don't. A spiritual process of healing takes place deep inside.

"...his Spirit is offered us at all times, in the events of each day, to make prayer spring up from us..." (Catechism #2659)

For spiritual issues: Examine yourself and compile an honest list of areas needing improvement (lack of prayer, lack of trust, disobedience...). Pray the issues through in tongues. Read scripture, then back in tongues.

For physical issues: Examine yourself and write down your issues (overweight, health problems, lack of exercise, lack of sleep, etc.). Pray the issues through in tongues. *"With all prayer and supplication, pray at every opportunity in the Spirit..."* (Ep 6:18).

For emotional issues: Examine yourself and write down your issues (fear, insecurity, withdrawal from relationships, anger, temptation...). Pray the areas through in tongues. (My booklet *True Confessions, prayers to heal the secrets in your soul*, would help with this process.)

Personal experience with emotional issues: I often find myself praying through emotions in tongues, whether it is fear, anger, sorrow, etc. If I need to cry, sometimes it comes out in tongues. In the psalms we find a broad expression of emotions. It makes sense to me, practically, to take these issues to the Lord in tongues because He gave us our emotions and we need to work them through so we can come to a place of praise.

"The need to involve the senses in interior prayer corresponds to a requirement of our human nature. We are body and spirit, and we experience the need to translate our feelings externally. We must pray with our whole being to give all power possible to our supplication." (Catechism #2702)

In temptation: When you are tempted to take a wrong path, read scriptures on taking the right path, repent, ask for help in tongues. It's resolve and grace, those important elements in the Sacrament of Reconciliation. *"Your ways, O Lord, make known to me; teach me your paths, guide me in Your truth and teach me…"* (Ps 25:4-5).

For enlightenment with scripture: Read a particular verse, ask for insight, and then pray in tongues. I pray *"…that the God of our Lord Jesus Christ, the Father of glory, may give you a spirit of wisdom and revelation resulting in knowledge* *of him. May the eyes of your hearts be enlightened, that you may know what is the hope that belongs to his call..."* (Eph 1:17-18).

Feeling stingy? Reflect on some scriptures on generosity, ask forgiveness for lack of generosity, then pray in tongues and ask the Lord for an opportunity to give. *"Tell them to do good, to be rich in good works, to be generous, ready to share"* (1Tm 6:18).

Feeling stubborn and self centered? Read scripture, ask for a docile generous spirit, go into tongues, back into scripture, and words. *"O Lord, open my lips, and my mouth shall proclaim your praise"* (Ps 51:17).

As intercession: When you don't know how to pray for a situation, lift it to the Lord in tongues.

Want to complain? A friend told me one time that I even complain in tongues. Well, it does help get out the negative, and who better to complain to but God?

For mental clarity: My mother used to pray, "Lord think through me today." Focus on the mind of Christ as you pray in tongues, to clear your head.

For damaged relationships: Ask the Holy Spirit to create an opportunity for repair of relationships, then pray in tongues. *"For he is our peace, he who made both one and broke down the dividing wall of enmity..."* (Eph 2:14).

Want to run away? Pray "Lord I have this temptation to leave when things get hard, instead of facing issues. Please help me." Try reading scripture, seek wise counsel, go to confession, go into tongues for wisdom, then talking, then back in tongues. *"A wise man's knowledge wells up in a flood, and his counsel, like a living spring"* (Sir 21:13).

Don't know how to love? Pray, "Lord, teach me to love." Talk, read scripture, go into tongues for guidance, then words. *"If I speak in human and angelic tongues, but do not have love, I am a resounding gong or a clashing cymbal"* (1Cor13:1).

Sick all the time? Pray, "Lord, teach me how to be well." Talk, read scripture, pray in tongues for insight, and back and forth.

More: Again, in this section I am just sharing my personal use of tongues. And always, it goes without saying, be appropriate, respectful of the environment. Pray out loud or silently in tongues, depending on circumstances. Try praying in tongues fifteen minutes a day for specific things, maybe five minutes for family concerns, five minutes for yourself.

Repeat reminder: Always begin and end with asking the Holy Spirit what He wants brought up and give it to Him at the end.

Use tongues often: The more you use it the more the gift will develop.

Is there more? Oh yes, I am sure, so much more. But this is what I feel led to include. There are many things I need to learn about the wonderful ways of the Holy Spirit with this gift of tongues. *"I have dealt with great things that I do not understand; things too wonderful for me, which I cannot know"* (Job 42:3).

8

Closing Prayer

"...grow in the grace and knowledge of our Lord and savior Jesus Christ. To him be glory now and to the day of eternity. Amen" (2 Pt 3:18).

"The Lord leads all persons by paths and in ways pleasing to him, and each believer responds according to his heart's resolve and the personal expressions of his prayer..." (Catechism #2699)

Heavenly Father, I lift to You all who have read this book. I pray that nothing shall interfere with what You desire to teach them. Please clear up any remaining confusion so they can truly hear from You in a deep and wonderful way.

Help them with the issues of their lives. Wake up their hearts to Your awesome love. Help them to trust, to experience spousal relationship with You. Help them enter into the wonderful purpose You have for them. Help them to repent, forgive, and watch Your Spirit move! Then help them to do it again!

Oh Father, You love them so very much. Do

something awesome in their lives as they move forward in this precious relationship with You. You in them, and them in You (1Jn 4:13). And Father, please fill in the gap between what You wanted them to receive through this book, and what I presented. In Jesus' Name I pray. Amen.

"May the God of peace...Jesus our Lord, furnish you with all that is good, that you may do His will. May he carry out in you what is pleasing to him through Christ Jesus, to whom be glory for ever and ever. Amen" (Heb 13:20).

9

Workshop possibilities

INTRODUCTORY: Precious Power Workshop
This is a one day easy introduction for parishes (or a three evening parish mission), using the format of my booklet *Precious Power, healing flows when we welcome, listen, empower*

This mini introduction to life in the Spirit could include:

The welcome of the Father
The listening heart of Jesus
The power of the Holy Spirit

FOR ALL LEVELS: Life in the Spirit Seminars
This is a seven week series with teaching sessions on God's love, salvation, new life, receiving God's gift, praying for baptism in the Holy Spirit, growth and transformation in Christ. Having the extended format gives people time to absorb and reflect on the topics.

ADVANCED: Power Tongues Work Groups

I have been hosting "power tongues work groups" in my home for several months. They have a two-fold objective:

    A. To coach and develop the gift of tongues in the individual; to develop the habit of using one's prayer tongue often throughout the day

    B. Praying this way as a group we edify and confirm each other at the same time we are accomplishing many spiritual things as God leads.

Format

1. We learn to deal with our personal issues before we begin and set them aside. If an issue keeps surfacing, we focus on it and pray it through in tongues.

2. We ask for a generous heart so we can seek God's prayer in faith, expressing what He wants us to pray for.

3. We have a new realization that it's 'not about me', but about what's on God's heart and what the body of Christ may need.

4. The extended prayer tongues requires physical stamina and a resolute determination to press on in faith even

though our minds may begin to wander or our spirits get weary. Often it's because we've overcome weariness and pushed through that the most power is manifest and prayers are most effective. (During the time in tongues it's important to have a 'coach' to exhort the participants to press on.)

5. Throughout the time in tongues the Lord directs us, much like an invisible orchestra director, and at some point we just end in unison. After we have stopped praying in tongues we share and make note of what people receive from the Lord. It's amazing how the visions and prayers of the individuals are in synch with each other. We confirm and build on each other's focus. There's a deep refreshing strengthening as we share.

6. There's no right or wrong way to do this, especially when a solid gathering prayer is prayed at the outset.

7. We end the time with a prayer that 'seals' in all that God has accomplished, and one that cleanses us from anything out of order that may have clung to us.

8. To recap: We begin with prayer, asking for the Holy Spirit to deepen and guide our prayer time. We take authority over any negative spirit activity that would interfere, and we invite the Lord to expand our understanding of and use of tongues. We pray in tongues until the Holy Spirit stops us. We share the words, visions, scriptures, prayers that the Lord brings forth during our tongues time. We close in prayer, remaining on time with a clear start and end time. (1 ½ hours from arrival to departure has been our timeframe.)

10

Resources

For general references on prayer: ***Catechism of the Catholic Church,*** Catholic Book Publishing Co, New York ISBN 0-89942-256-x.

The New Life in the Spirit Seminar Manual, available from the National Service Committee of the Catholic Charismatic Renewal, Chariscenter USA, Box 628, Locust Grove VA 22508 www.nsc-chariscenter.org.

Charisms, Ed. Sr. Mary Anne Schaenzer, SSND, www.nsc-chariscenter.org.

As By A New Pentecost, by Patti Gallagher Mansfield, available from the author at www.ccrno.org.

God loves you, and there's nothing you can do about it (Saying yes to the Holy Spirit) by David Mangan, Servant Books, www.ServantBooks.org.

Sober Intoxication of the Spirit by Raniero

Cantalamessa, O.F.M. Cap., Servant Books, www.ServantBooks.org.

Healing in the Spirit of Jesus by Fr.Peter Sanders, C.O. www.newpentecost.org.

Because I have been helping Christians develop their testimonies, written and oral, on the working of the Holy Spirit in their lives, I am including two current references:

Shelly Currin's **"*From the Shadows...and into His marvelous light*"** shellycurrin@shadowstolight.net.

Theresa Huether's ***"I'm Singing a New Song...Striving for Authentic Life in Christ"*** theresahuether@gmail.com.

Order Form

All of Linda Schubert's resource materials can be ordered online at www.linda-schubert.com.

To order using the form below, send payment to Linda Schubert, Miracles of the Heart Ministries, P.O. Box 4034, Santa Clara, CA 95056; Fax (408) 734-8661, Phone (408) 734-8663, E-mail linda@linda-schubert.com.

Books

____	*Precious Power** .... $ 3.00	____
____	*True Confessions** .... $ 3.00	____
____	*Miracle Hour** .... $ 3.00	____
____	*Miracle Moments** .... $ 3.00	____
____	*Rich in Mercy** .... $ 3.00	____
____	*Miracle Man Handbook** .... $ 3.00	____
____	*Miracle Woman Handbook** .... $ 3.00	____
____	*Healing Power of a Father's Blessing* .... $ 3.50	____
____	*Five Minute Miracles* .... $ 4.95	____
____	*Transfigurations, Places of Prayer with*	
	Prof. R. England $20.00	____
____	*The Gift of Tongues*** .... $ 4.00	____

CD's

____	Miracle Hour Prayers	
	(Pray along with Linda) .... $ 8.00	____
____	Double CD Teaching and Miracle Hour Prayers $14.00	____
____	Receive the Gift	
	(Linda's song in English and Spanish)................. $8.00	____

Total	$ _____
California residents add 9.25% tax	$ _____
***Shipping	$ _____
TOTAL ENCLOSED	$ _____
U.S. FUNDS	

Visa _____ Mastercard _____

Name on card _____

Expiration date _____

Card # _____

Ship to _____

_____

_____

Phone_____

*For quantity discount of *True Confessions, Miracle Moments, Rich in Mercy, Miracle Hour, Precious Power, Miracle Man Handbook or Miracle Woman Handbook,* use the following chart:

1-25 copies	....	$3.00 each
26-50 copies	....	2.75 each
51-99 copies	....	2.25 each
100+ copies	....	1.75 each

**For quantity discount of *The Gift of Tongues,* use the following chart:

1-25 copies	....	$5.00 each
26-50 copies	....	4.75 each
51-99 copies	....	4.25 each
100+ copies	....	3.75 each

Bookstores order Five Minute Miracles from Catholic Book Publishing Co., 77 West End Road, Totowa, NJ 07512, Phone (973) 890-2400. For other books, standard trade discount applies.

***For media rate shipping to U.S. locations, refer to chart below:

1 to	5 items	add $2.50
6 to	20 items	add $3.50
21 to	35 items	add $4.50
36 to	50 items	add $5.50
51 to	70 items	add $6.50
71 to	100 items	add $7.50
100+ items	add $8.50 per 100	

If you want to schedule Linda for a retreat or workshop,
write, phone or e-mail
Linda Schubert
Miracles of the Heart Ministries
P.O. Box 4034, Santa Clara, CA 95056
Phone (408) 734-8663 • Fax (408) 734-8661
www.linda-schubert.com
linda@linda-schubert.com